The Chicken Coop Scoop

Written by Helen Dineen

Illustrated by Stephen Stone

Collins

Flora is keen to be a reporter.

"I can do that," thinks Flora with glee.

She scoots off at speed.

Elspeth is scattering grain in the brown soil.

"This is not a scoop!" frowns Flora.

Bree is training. She hoists logs.

"This is not a scoop!" frowns Flora.

Splash! Blair is dripping wet.

"This is not a scoop!" frowns Flora, and her tail droops.

Flora trails back to the roost. She hears cracking in the corner.

7

It is not a chicken egg. A crowd starts to form and they point in alarm.

Can it be a monster egg? Flora is not afraid. She creeps up.

As the egg cracks, Elspeth, Blair and Bree agree to run.

Flora swoops in. She has now got her thrilling scoop!

What a splendid scoop! Flora is the star of the roost.

Flora's dragon snap

But her stardom is short.

"Bad dragon," Flora groans. "You are
a spoilsport!"

Map

✿ Review: After reading ✿

Use your assessment from hearing the children read to choose any GPCs, words or tricky words that need additional practice.

Read 1: Decoding

- Look through the book. What words can the children find with the adjacent consonants "s" "t"? (*hoists, roost, starts, monster, star, stardom*)

Read 2: Prosody

- Model reading each page with expression to the children.
- After you have read each page, ask the children to have a go at reading with expression, thinking about how Flora is feeling and therefore how she might say the words.

Read 3: Comprehension

- Turn to pages 14 and 15 and ask the children to retell the story in their own words, using the pictures as prompts.
- For every question ask the children how they know the answer. Ask:
  o What job is Flora keen to do? (*be a newspaper reporter*)
  o Elspeth is scattering grain – why isn't this a scoop? (*it isn't exciting enough, it's an everyday activity*)
  o Why do Elspeth, Blair and Bree run away when the egg starts hatching? (*they are frightened, it might be a monster*)
  o What was Flora's thrilling scoop? (*a dragon egg hatching in the chicken coop*)